DATE DUE

ALSO BY LARRY EIGNER

Poems (1941)
From the Sustaining Air (1953)
Look At the Park (1958)
On My Eyes (1960)
The Music, the Rooms (1965)
Six Poems (1967)
Another Time In Fragments (1967)
The-/ Towards Autumn (1967)
Air the Trees (1968)
The Breath of Once Live Things In the Field With Poe (1968)
A Line That May Be Cut (1968)
Clouding (1968)
Flat and Round (1969 and corrected edition 1980)
Farther North (1969)
Valleys Branches (1969)
Circuits - A MICROBOOK (1971)
Looks Like Nothing/ The Shadow/ Through Air (1972)
Selected Poems (1972)
Words Touching Ground Under (1972)
What You Hear (1972)
Shape Shadow Elements Move (1973)
Things Stirring Together Or Far Away (1974)
Anything on Its Side (1974)
Suddenly/ it gets light/ and dark in the street (1975)
My God/ The Proverbial (1975)
The Music Variety (1976)
Watching/ how or why (1977)
The World and Its Streets, Places (1977)
Cloud, invisible air (1978)
Flagpole/ Riding (1978)
Country/ Harbor/ Quiet/ Act/ Around - selected prose (1978)
Heat simmers cold & (1978)
Lined up bulk senses (1979)
Time/ details/ of a tree (1979)
Now there's/ a morning/ hulk of the sky (1981)
Earth Birds (1981)
Waters/ Places/ A Time (1983)

LARRY EIGNER

WATERS/ PLACES/ A TIME

EDITED BY ROBERT GRENIER

BLACK SPARROW PRESS
SANTA BARBARA 1983

PS
3509
I47
W39
1983

ACKNOWLEDGEMENT

Poems in this book have appeared previously in the following small books/booklets: *A Line That May Be Cut; Cloud; Invisible Air; Earth Birds; Earth Ship 8; Flagpole Riding; My God The Proverbial; Sparrow 13; The Music Variety; Tottel's 15; Valleys Branches*

anthologies: *A Controversy of Poets* (Doubleday Anchor); *Poems Now* (Kulchur Press); *The Gist of Origin* (Grossman); *The New American Poetry, 1945-1960* (Grove Press); *Thunderbolts of Peace and Liberation* (BB Bks)

tape: "around new / sound daily / means" (S Press Tonbandverlag)

magazines: *Ann Arbor Review; Athanor; Big Deal; Blank Tape; Camels Coming; Caterpillar; Chelsea; Coyote's Journal; Curtains; European Judaism; Flute; Gay Sunshine; Hills; Imago; Interstate; Klactoveedsedsteen; La-Bas; Living Hand; Mother; New Student Review; Old West Review; Origin; Orogrande; Poetry* (April, 1966, "the earth you may as well. . ."); *Poetry Now; Pyramid; Renegade; Roof; Shell; Stony Hills; Text; The; The Capilano Review; The Ear in a Wheatfield; The Paris Review; The Outsider; The South Florida Poetry Journal; This; Tish; Webster Review; Wild Dog; Winter; Zahir.*

LIBRARY OF CONGRESS CATALOGING IN PUBLICATION DATA

Eigner, Larry, 1927-
    Waters, places, a time.

    I. Grenier, Robert. II. Title.
PS3509.I47W39 1983   811'.54   82-24359
ISBN 0-87685-498-6 (signed ed.)
ISBN 0-87685-497-8 (pbk.)

TABLE OF CONTENTS

WATERS / PLACES / A TIME

co-op

wind

ows a

door

Whoppers Whoppers Whoppers!

memory fails

these are the days

the sound

        sea through the horizon
    under the stand of trees

it comes by on the wind

   flat and round
   earth and sky

motion unperceived   thought
that the visible should be
  this sun   standing water as
stretching the lawn
  day really endless time
  would change   broad air
    the branches turning the hulls
                        condense the docks
        far away   stir of waves
                    makes light   you hear
            cut sound from
              the other afternoons

              so drowned
                          and
        all sleeping may be a mood

flock of birds
a moment
of one tree reached

apples fall to the ground

a quiet staircase

pelting

where is rain

rubber boots

to see the ocean
  peace and quiet in the sky
  drown view of the city

you imagine the reach of noise
  the expanse to hear the sound

    the sea echoes wind
     long against man

        and through the streets salestalk
     precise, acoustics

       glass glass gas gas
        coloring eyes
       a system of motion

         darkness blowing a wall
                cracked in most cases
      foam stars
         as in the air as
         under wheels
          of feet

       as leaves still growing in
        fewer millions

     imagination eating
      time like a body
    mountains on water
       wave over and over
     vivid on gray
    striding streets at
    once all that looms

if you find time
    you think

if a few things
    merge, you may sleep

　　　　　　trees
light　　flying one leg

　　birds in　the leaves
　　which thick sound
　　　　　　　ready ready ready, will

　　　　　stream away

　　　　　　or a taste
　　　quiet, smelling of height

things more or less
in a Yogi's dream

voluntary

how much the moon may be

the wind

different

places

thinking

men forms

variously

size

the thickness

like statues

out back

round earth

square miles

between poles

imagine

upside down

polynesia

caves

radio track

dishes

to hear dim stars

the sky a field

sheep

horses

mines

cities everywhere

on the eyeballs

particles

deserts

streams

the oceans curve

piss, for one thing

to make things go

muggy

and the foghorn

clear air

darkening

wherever from

cars with red lights

plane tails corners

there was nothing

buildings stand for years

thought back on

stars

flash the wind

                    down the rain

          thunder cry arrives

one minute

                    dogs

                              bark

reticent

being

stand

the lamp

by the window

it's the rear face

of the corner house

far off, the sky

darkening

big trees, tops wild

space look

direction

some time of air

cars

on the road

far off

night turned

look

raise up

the dead

the sun comes

the earth goes

how many trees

motions gathering

imperceptible

birds

drive

hungry

settle

tides

creeks stem

the intersection

2 levels

out the window

a fall still of night

in back and ahead

some distance
around,   round,   round

as there has to be

enough   tunnel mouth

gears

traffic

various climb

lights

the places to go

whatever there's been

in constancy

through the day

the fog holds
    the light darts
  poured into it
        you know the excitement

    cars on the road

    the rain passes

open road

you look in houses

and the night sky

any place

is all one

this time

you never know
what is the group
what picks it up

A s l e e p

mummied

what space there

is was

snow

flakes
are single

down

to earth

but they light

on others

or a tree

living still the

current of air

the sun diffuses

some steepness

however close

twigs

it first snowed

a while back

begin a
mid things
the wind
          barely says

     up and down

          the house

          wall

               corners

shadowy

gesticulations

on the lawn

young tree
trunks
a little in the sun

leaf
shapes
across them too

beautiful

the light is

all one way

after

noon

where it falls

most of the earth

unknown

to us

clouds are idle

spaces

another plane is
gas   far, a lot, the night

shadows too

the fish tank bubbles

everything stand

continue shapes

the end of a film

everybody's serious

in the "ballroom"

"dancing"

the dead
light
the walls
no stream but
the union
things are
the wonder
tree

thing see now
pole corner
front moon sliced
sun

catch light shadow

a screen flopped
loose

it was one of those blizzards, one
on another

the shadow of slow
day
passes

the gulls flying around
ruddering balance

the wind lit

eastward it seems

maybe it's the stars
a little lower at night

a broken-up plane   there is
touch   sea

there is
the wind

I was disappearing   into the sunshine

you live the

hopeful
life

to see
depth to the moon

piano and strings

the wind and rain

go together

quite a time

shadow

valley

thickly

filled up

lands

a dark day

all this time

clouds

birds in

the air

and it rains

trees

a few leaves

with

stand

the flock

   on the ground

slant

 wire

   air flickers

 clouds approach

  now

  some stars
       seem close

      in the branches all
          the motion   visible

      mass

          the sea gathers

          a little further

              sound

   the glint in the water

  the corners

 you make as

   the lines straighten

42

the sound

in its reach

cold

north
is

it ended

now or

something

different

meaning

the faces set

to play music

beautiful throat

the ungainly man

controls

it is music   he
become 5 men
    in a line
        nor any man

          to see   time,

      delight of the mind

    in time, the
    harmony

           at once, going

     a jungle, strange   more
      performance with the lips

Environ s

Many shapes of wings
on the sky and the table;
and large men carefully at dusk
lengthened by lights   watering their lawns

turn, paterfamilias

 and the sweet hay as I go
 from one foot to the other
more so than I might
mingled with barber's tonic
from the morning's shops
 of papers and bright rag
  as if we could
  take time out for life

and the afternoon's seas, like yards

At some smell of smoke
I found a spray behind me
and the two on my right gone
 tending the grass, all night
everyone beautifully
 (by themselves   the same thing

time   for the surroundings

  against the strip of hill
 ending low, a space
 on this side, hut for clouds

HOTRODS

so the same

space

there   houses

as the day's

quiet

you ride for some hours

stalagmites

clouds   cities

L o w

startling idea
of the small car

Do you think you might ever walk again

but convertible too
necking   soft hats   a deck
like between sleeps
tangent beaches

Ride any place in the sky
when you look by

moments

invisible wheels

shadow along the trees

now

here

too

elsewhere

what

next

clouds

down

beyond the sky

and one

gust

what damp paper
wood foggy day
rain countering glass
    little
        wind
     brought on down
             articulate
      equally, the sea
         may sound in leaves

curtains

shades

the ocean
          and the sky

both deep

hills

the music of

the sea

beyond

the wood

the wind blows

the leaves

they stay

there   such times

roots spread

flower

face   the sky

sphere

ah the seed

not to choose

Air

                f o r

in the yard of

                S a m

another house

                B o r a s h

a phone bell

miles away

in
doors

a small willow
by the front steps

white clouds in the sky

far from these birds and green

the most sunshine

empty but still
trashbarrels
back of the porch

lattice

the cool dirt

shadow cast under

clamp puffing quartered cigar
as he mows
the grass

to be odd business

power that's noise

"high society"
               so
comes what song off
           the breeze down

sounds
　　quiet

down

　the streets

　　　range

　　lost

　　big

　　city

　　the earth taken

　　　corners

　　　　what does

　　　　sometime

　　　round　and
　　　　　　wide

　　　one and another

ashes

fire

light

mass

the moon

   in

  the
    sky
     after visiting

  the wire

   the wind flows

sounded like

must have been ocean

in the summer autumn
football crowds

in india like trees
open and shut

some way to be occupied

woman or man from
the beach

feet

arms the

warm air

passing home shoes

on steady

to be heard

off recently

dried

the trees will

be here

at night

once in a while still

you want

another child

churchbells

years ago

minutes

while storms of men, say,

last night, some

freshness of tack,

not to believe,

nothing but war

is war, ex-

haustive death, a wind

rain, starlight's gone

blue, nothing alone, birds sing

a cat
   stops
      there

dirt
the breeze

   tree shadows
      clear of sun

to find

the weight

of things

the fish

the air

support

the flower
in the earth
pot

the woods

the floors

insect

  leaf

    shadows

      on the wall

        soon be icy

      accurate

        dawn returns

          in the picture frames

        reflections

           due to the wind moving

          far away heats

            the sun so often
              as it blots trees
              lights up the panes

driftwood

the sands

a tree spreads

dirt is

hard grains

in the trees

the strength of cross

winds

and then sunlight

in the shadow

cross

winds

sunlight

the force

    crash of a car

accordion

streetlights

    dimmer than day

      they were burning all night

stars

    it's raining

siren

    people look
        in the wind

  fire's

      bigger than ambulance

         and now the fantastic cold

           come back from there

             what's time counted not

             slower quiet the snow

           windows

            chimney

            smoke going up

            the middle   air

             the bulk   cloudy

Winter

3 black figures

in the street

all
　　turn out

to be
　　schoolgirls

a car horn

briefly

how far

does

the power

failure

go   what

flashed
black

how much could they
    flicker

  pull down

  the shades on them

  the lights burning

    night

    distance

like stores, banks

secure skies

disparate   earth

tight   curving

dark moon

all somehow by the eyes

still known

children

bring

home

work

to learn

heavy busses

the world already

playing together

The days the motors burn past
the houses , under the trees

repair smoke   your

shingles

all grade 5 on
the beach trip   in a bunch

teachers

whistle

steady

heat

slow

map

calendars

if you see it
might be
easy

how
anyone works

in the haze

The jets   jet
    black pail the air

            fingers   sudden   back size

            in sound

            furnaces clear
        the wings

    when you walk you fall

            to stand you on your head

dive
  over
        loop in the world

    quivering

        straight
                angstroms

                            how no volt
                        the unexpected
                            they race

            a peacefully foaming sea

        death   to
            the ramp

                    is gone

parking lot but

there are words otherwise

and here's a recording shop

something to eat then

dog with bone

corners at times

buildings sopped   by-products

through some range of goods

weird? is

it mystery? enough?

fish in the museum

pavement mosaic

as yet in the river too

far off turned

earth matter   blocks   brick

your eye sighting level

a city fixed in the ash

likewise come by the air

slender

dream architecture

opening a garden wall

such hundreds of years suddenly

stop pain cut fate

as they've said

1 time there were no roads

(anyplace) and

here these people are

glad to have
these copies of things
after a while

microphones

on top of the world

heads spin
empty

glad to have
these copies of things
after a while

microphones

on top of the world

heads spin
empty

perfect
strangers,   dining
in the air   together

tossed   out
the window   the world

Gluttony deeper
Lust

as plate keeps
precarious
trays in

and there are
delicates still
areas such
foot travel

aisles lead
ramp taxi
foundations off

cats turning
al-
leys to sleep

in
light   the

earth seems

to run

gotta go

ta la

most thing

roam legs

novel experience

get stuck

vertical direction

make and break

distances

smelly roof

ride over

to the walls raised the
works

face people, their panes, the poor

food brought through the mouth

dichotomy

young

old

around

where

gunmen

deflect

bound to drown

enough

stakes other

fantastic

sums

out of mind

tend to your business

Who's intelligent

Who's articulate

at hands

shorter and shorter words

on and up the tower

—————

Aggre-
gates

pow!

sail

dark

air

the night

Arrangements

pistons
products

the straight
ways   wide

space

Not the same

Nothing

is

ever   there
are forces
among things

like in clocks
mass measures

how many a neighborhood

stairs   shelves

up   and down

there are still mice

what's in the closet

put away

dark the

how long
and wide

do graveyards dissolve
in the out
doors

the air brings
    rain
  shifts with heat

there's no such thing as
identical

all right

the end of a day

5 & ½ million
           trees
annual for the
           T i m e s
    how much is that a
wood pile
    could not be so
high   who numbers
    streams   beaten out
        the anvil
            makes good
        work   how many
            leaves or is
        it branches?   comparisons
            are themselves   incidentals
            in determining what
                to afford   speak
                    the outsides of the
                possible?   what
                        goes by   girders have
                such multiple holes
                    brinks in
                    all-round space and
                outline   there are things I
                    won't get over   how much
                                green backs?
                    the curved earth
                    holds white clouds
                    or black, or grey
                        before stars
                    variety
                        in a jungle while
                    in a stand of pine
                        a spruce is rare

89

a dead-letter office
    is designated somewhere in this
    complex
        well ruled

    colors for sale to eat in
    these stores

        dark glasses

shadows of planes in
    enough space

    shadow of cloud

    the sun shines brilliantly

grief   dry the

        council

    far away

  inveterate   interest

     some dust

       the stars are a million pieces

          some million a million

        people suffer the end

High piled
clouds and

leveled   we go fast

above   how much to

can we think

I could well go back to
                    no drink

and all that fuel
stored on the ground

for which the
demand is
rising

unexpectedly

cross   recross

the stewardesses
freeze in water
bare knees
hanging around
ordinarily
for 1 thing are
good for the pilots I
suddenly thought

casualness in
    so many causes

everybody does

otherwise

they would not

look

ok

the earth continues
or comes to a stop

what time is
   it day

   I may
 sleep

 hour on hour
or all the time, what
   a consideration, you
 pretty good,
      what a question   forwards in
         a circle the
      other way around it
            may
         have gone, the thought
            of what to do   a tree
         sits and birds come
            there's a word for each leaf, and each wall and

      a word for nothing

(resting or doing something
Southern California, Feb.9 '71)
highway

low in the wind

breaks   open

as buildings   in

places   or varying masses,

binds, to keep each other on the move

oil and water

empty spaces

and many things piled up

the

underground

seeing or

belief

smell

you hear something

what's a dense field

what tides

and the air takes the sun

deep as it is

broken cement

all through the town

lumps

earth smell

out of the wind

no, flowers

pots

next in the cellar

rubbish

all over it

took a bit

to fix it in space

there's movies

like two billboards

the most beautiful

up in the night

towards the sky

can't hear them

you go and get

a donut

framed in glass

some things drunken

all customers visible

hazy weather

plied walls

known

often

soft stars

winds

e.g.

modern times

is full of

museums

3 / 4   t i m e

put yr teeth together and see if it fits comfortably

ending the dentist

at least a while

when I take you out in the surrey a little
                              with the fringe on top

―――――
―――――

DOWN ON THE BED you

can't

imagine

enough

how you
stand

for your
self

one quarter
the muscles
the face

mouth

changes

the

frosted car

I imagine

hearing the motor

of the girl who lives here

or next door

upstairs

now

the snow heavy

hours

such days

that's it

news

what

drives away

the world

There is no community

he goes to

Work   mornings

the motor fades sway the

numberless   towns

museum or

the endless insides of the store

take something home to
alter the window

close
　　-up

　　what

　　　O

　　　happens

　　　　pervades

　　　　the world

　　　　scene

　　　　channel where

　　　　　you don't think

　　　　　the wind

　　　　　lights

　　　　　fire

　　　　　shadows

　　　　　the sun

one died by this tremendous headache
drowning in laughter
the tv was a gas
some kind of vacation in the wards
        then many went down and voted

            the whole year round
        stars frosty or something
                wonderful view
            at the edge of your seat

        the moon off
            polluted waters
                    degrees merge
                miles
                clear sunday

                the one-round fight
            everybody watched
            they had expectations
            chew it , it
                can drop

            tomorrow morning

    romance of the moon

            across curtain, strings
                    plaster different from panes
            an even coat of paint

just outside

scaffold flutes on the sill

?
you like to come down and watch

the gym

with the sick men

I know what it's like

not to get dizzy looking down

the painter comes through the window
to paint
the doorknob

sparrows gather on the chimney
perhaps cold   later

beating safely overhead

come around
night and day

oil
shellfish beds

this business to keep clear
a little further

various in the wind

flat sky
     going down
  to leaves

birds river
    sounds

what then
moon's like

   is

     looks

   still

the face of death

think

you

numerous

not seen

the mind

season to season

Pigeons   the
  heavy rain suddenly
begins
            silences
between the box-cars
            rails

    levels
            the round clock ticking

  what blood
    lifts it up

visiting   yesterday
today burying

half an hour
    out

death   part of life
        because it's strange it makes

the sun yield

        stars swamped by the day

    the night open
wind

        and cars roll
    blankets   outside
        lawns
                    the past wanders

    how many people
        along brief buildings

                lights
        in all waters

    that you should see
    the mist   warm

        on metal   the snow
        wets moss

    of the sweated wall

112

that the ground,   spooks,
        and uneven

    the buildings cast shadows

    even as the bakery
                its smell

    and the tree next door
            is close

It grows   dissolve
        the wind

            turn around
            in the air

history is for tourist

addition

houses   ages and sizes

store

cats

corners

the wind

people

going by

that's all figures
the car volume more sun

a gull coasting

the porch

going along alone

straight roads

poles march

name gradations
the skies far no angle
above the signs
or how many   that make
the maximum

what lights are there
before stars

to think all the time

spokes

these fumes
it's
mirrors that tilt
things

the curb round fender

hard now immobile lids

inside down and outside up
morning whole cat poring the cup

the gray sea what seasons

strength feels

babies   how

unconscious we are   startling

big men on the way

they run   they

can't walk far   decline

the mountain grass   just look at

stars   knock-outs

how slow is the distance
                        the graves

the strong green

complicated productions

the loudspeaker from the field

covers the street

the phone seemed too simple

the old man's idea

he wants to go there

cutting the grass with gas

leaves rising and falling
in what winds

a new
  ballgame

   paper is fresh
      under arms

    the street to
      be sudden

       front

     right, it's

    smooth driving

     smooth walking

       parked

      a crowd

        the sea

     always retreats

           there
            ahead

       always

          comes on

      resonances

     a few garages

         earshot

119

different

times

birds

the wind

sound

from leaves

the moon

is

miles from the air

trans
formed?

Break the dogfight

the lawnmower too
            up
the rollercoaster

as the lark flew
    the field plane

a sudden sky
you hold in distinction

            roots grow
        into a blade or stalk

the railway

the children
grimed precision
    who will
    be men

    the crickets
    do not keep me
        from nothing

the afternoon has many hours

passengers take the air
    the shut deck
as if looking through the sea

              the rattle of boats and

    the great clock figure
                 a spire
              rides over

         (the inrolled
                      maps in the sky

         the parishes

           the sea
             is turned up
                          and fed

the two lights in
unison the
    daytime

    sides of the road

    birds fly

        the moving wind

rainy

days

hours

nights

whenever

the trees stop

the sun solid
        ground it soaks

what bird took

wing

a minute ago

now there are others

some white stuff

they eat and build

farther

there an ample world

in which

their sounds are quiet

a bird
bath a cloud
dropped
gathered
mass to a place

leaning
tree

stars   out

Out of the wind   and leaves

first rustle

the rain straight

down

the wall within

the wall of sound

to open your ears
real music

on the wire sparrows

or any other birds
sit still

their world dimensional

more than dogs or cats
or perhaps men

and listen

a moment of stillness

stick in the ear

a beginning and origin

attachment
of flight

before the sea's exertion
to trace the appearing moon

or stormy as it may be

an afternoon rain

how long it can seem to last

I think it's over there
    the sky through the trees

I recall passing through them, many

branches and leaves too
    begin   time

    is present

        the moon increases night
        water   sparingly

a new fathom

        a table   crickets
            unendingly surface

        the field out back

        different tympanum

            I imagine it shining

                    the far bliss   home
                    in the risen sun,   the country

            the stream like a serpent, or fish

                              to go down

                    the harbor teeming
                    with broad flats   but then

                    the horizon

                              trailing back

            the merrygoround in the park
            away from the slips

                the horn goes off to the piccolo

                        the thunder mists

                    moving up a course

angelic youth
found home

the stepwise leaves
finally rattle

days follow   days
raking   slight wing

morning the sun rises

brick corners the evergreen pool

you see a mirror through glass

sky half
up the staircase
the other way

the trees sound of a river
birds still hold

while the river bends
visible from the plane
fuming
continues after takeoff

almost a bird answering the dog

a hole in the clouds moves

the hole in the sky

great multiple
time   bare
    track
        a line
of clear windows

    a space set
            the city
        yard
        jaws
                of music   continual waste

        a vast pine
                the town
            room for woods

        how much could you place in the sky

        the river
    what's your shape

                dust floating around   how many
                    thrust down
                        to final seconds

                    as if under the boards
                        mounting papers

        days and nights lower
            beside roots in the earth
                close off the winter, like death

the splits you go in

the rounds of idea

the panels vaulting

teeth or diamond eyes
confronted in the street

Sibelius,   shaking like the rain

the vibrations wet
relief
there's narrow joining

or some book   you move on   seas

the hillsides of the past

the mouths of burrows   light

Washing between the buildings
      Holland   the clear sky
         over the hay-loading
            the clouds'
               brief rise a temperate substance

as if the white mortar of history
      the grounds of people   canals
         mirror the overhung banks   dividing
            bridges   and is water deep what
               opens the roots as calm

                        oblong

            even the streets are shining

         What happened
                  to fire, the clouds
      out of hand,   the machines'
            free fall,   sewers
               fouled up,   accuracy
                  of destructive laws

      Measure of bridges,   into the endless boats of water with
      those who would waste

                  monument to the underground

         suicide, and the reckless   put it off
               to the next moment

                     quiet

fog
roof of trolleys
cobbled
floods

night

mills like a tiller

varying distance of wind

Palestrina from
        invisible source

            voices

             time

        relays

            firecrackers

                independence

            the wind moves
                the trees streets

europe a map

a moment

on the wall

                f o r

chagall soaring

              B a r r y

self-portrait

            W a t t e n

has that town

settled smoke

from

here

to the world

values

steal

out of sight

how come

the year of the dragon

in some places

asteroids there are

countless

as sand

in hamburg

rhenish

at first

sound

complete

how many languages how many languages how many languages my
mind changed

    the efficacy of words

   member of earth and air
maple or pine a
  being a cat

    ambled width of the road

   ducks under
     the big car

    shadows thrusts in the wind

   facing another
     snout to snout

    the sunlight in the fur

  depth riding some puddle

      birds sit
      with trees

     what are
      the hairs

      riffling
      back to the tail

    3 bulbs burn down the hall
    through the front door

along walls

reached you

figure things

the solid

the group

life

span

the world where

energy goes out

binds

displaced

settling

near and far

develop touch

the wide awake

what

to study with

radio

in the common

light

why

go to town

if

your earth home

then dis

appears

watch out

for the streetlamp

listen 10

times a day to

the silence

before you (can) reach

any foreign part   or

more than one place

—————

for

James

Sherry

Little finger suddenly
not so small
        pretty far
fifty years old
        its bone big anyway

life to language
        and back   and forth
there's the walk to the store
        seen through leaves
the corner   fitful
        wind   space   branches

snow come a week ago
piled up
empty
        sky overhead
            or clouds

the sun shining

===

"I was glad that my missile had
been thrown away"
—Lord Jim   ch.9

mirrors scattered

you lie down

the sky is clear

or the dark various an

event in your eye

the winds come to your ear

how small each

arrow   what rooms pumped

with sounds may be

shut lids

beyond floors

birds sleep in the bush

good and bad

time goes

leaves changing shadows

the wind fails   what paths

I fight nothing
there are no weapons

separate clouds

traveling   in the years

the sun, depths,
varying, mass

so muggy

in the thread

sound

night

siren

and way back

away

when

place to place

well

life is

moving

like the wind

now

blowy

vacuum and weight

anything

at all   there

see mountain

shoulders, confusion

crowds of men

borne away

when you slow down there's sound
the ropes buffeted

against the flagstaffs

rest area

many placards

and walls hold

gravelly like rain

it may be dust

at

the base of the car

vacation

cabins

in the morning

all over

you realize

the trees above tall

swaying

steep up the hill lines

there's a good view

a road sign later

fast you can stop
and eat

it's motionless enough

and the sunshine

a bicyclist along the way

changing

certain months for years

here you live

    a massed game

        every week

      organization

       it takes spirit
           a

         wholesome thing

        stars

         come out

      the sun

           the streets dim rain

         the trees as if bared
         to light
              and dark space

life

night

goes by

hate

hiding with pillow

those guns

before

they

come to

your own ears

Beethoven

writing

hours

All matter

standing

build   up

wave to wave

the reality behind
the sky the
branches

wind   roots   seed   the tree

spread

merge

slide

if not

now when for

ever

through the

parts

patterning

eye in

time enough

fall of a leaf
　　in June

　this quiet tree rocks

　　　tangled winds, their places

　　calm beach, on the rough

　　clouds above the pace

　　　of any clocks, echo

　　some calls, burn

　smell cast

in the sun
　　　the bird
　　landing
　　　its shadow it

　　came over a roof

　　slowing to a branch

　　the light shifting

around here

last year's pink
poison   a notice
     the wind howled
yesterday ,   blew up the tide
     beyond the sky-line from trees
     through branches   even more
                    the days before

               out of
          the bark   clear half
          the garage trellis
             two arms of the vine
          tack   crossed way over

               the bare
          sun filling the air
          the roof melting snowcap
             down water   past
          summer,   with the rays
             some angle eventually
                slips through
          the flow

                    the inferred motion
                    from the continuous, your eyes

               followed, or being
                    dance

          the remainder was good

          the two windows shook

and an outer stream on the
house drainpipe

covering a side

those folds
leak   point of the exit

—————

hour minute hands seconds

Pound on the door
    it's our house
like clockwork
    go in and out
        cities are flooded, fall,
    everywhere is a place

        tree line wall

        porch window

        face

        corner

        branch form

        climates build
                various   circles

            over and round the earth

        flies pause at the ceiling

        or above a chair

            sleep solid

        wild shadows

                same thing and
                what else

the earth you may as well
   sit with a foot on the roof
     imagine how rain in the rain
       brief music can be

     piano open as
       eye   the sun
   never going off
                       or different times different
                         music of water
       as the snow melts
         carried through the mountain
           the sun   has made it white
       your bowstring avoids the steeple, it
         stands clear, as the moon
           at night in crowds
                       your body spread down before
                         clouds
                       a gradual loosening
           where the greater hill rises
             hard as your eyes belly
               cold houses as in heaven

           round around warm lights
                             upside down
                   encroach the sky

         tree disproportionate
           bush flower standing
             in front of your knee   you
               ride behind   the other
                 the broad accessory tapping
                   rain on the roof   nothing
                     inside that could be mistaken
                       the clouds are light

160

holding nothing but mist
in the deepening sky   I
would imagine it's
the single-roomed house you've lived in

flowers

passing on, white

Head full
of birds   the languages
of the world
    switching the scenery   the same
old things

a crow   momentary
    thicknesses of the air
are hills   shadows
    below waver
    some clearness   now these trees

        level the lawn
        across the street

    the sun there
            shift the world up out

            whistle in snow

Printed February 1983 in Santa Barbara & Ann Arbor
for the Black Sparrow Press by Graham Mackintosh
& Edwards Brothers Inc. Design by Barbara Martin.
This edition is published in paper wrappers;
there are 200 hardcover copies numbered & signed by
the author; & 26 copies handbound in boards by
Earle Gray lettered & signed by the author.

LARRY EIGNER was born in early August 1927 (got cerebral palsy then, is non-ambulatory) on Massachusetts Bay near Salem and Marblehead, north of Boston, south of Gloucester, and lived there till at the end of August '78 he came west to settle (?) in Berkeley. How and/or how much things (can be got to) go together (work) is some mystery.

Odd enough too, as puzzles go, that things are or can be given meaning or realized, by voice, emphasis, physical force—though without man there'd hardly be any meaning or intention, just as there would be no eyesight beyond the animal kingdom. (Meaning within bounds of what's actual, or at times in extending knowledge of it, as with physical and astronomical research.) And if we don't like to get too close to a star, for instance, we don't like getting too far away from one, in our heads, either.

Near and far—wide and narrow. Your neighborhood and how much of the world otherwise. Beginning ending and continuing. As they come, what can things mean? Briefly enough. What weights, imports? Nothing is ever quite as obvious as anything else, at least in context. A poem can't be too long, anything like an equatorial superduper highway girdling the thick rotund earth, but is all right and can extend itself an additional bit if you're sufficiently willing to stop anywhere.

A quick enough flashback makes things new

travel

how much

stand still

Photo: Debra Heimerdinger